Punctuation Celebration

by

ELSA
KNIGHT
BRUNO

illustrated by

JENNY
WHITEHEAD

Christy Ottaviano Books
HENRY HOLT and company
New York

Field Day Frolic

On your marks!

Get set!

Let's go!

To a sporty exploration

Into words and punctuation.

We'll meet the players, learn each name,

And celebrate this special game.

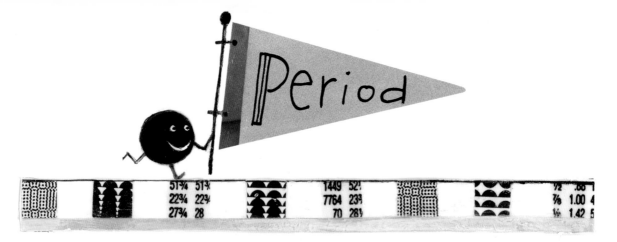

Period

The period is just a dot
Found sitting in its favorite spot.
When a sentence ends, it comes and plops,
And where it plops, the sentence STOPS.

It also can abbreviate
An address, first name, size, or weight
(Like lb. for pound, ft. for feet,
Doz. for dozen, and St. for street).

Elizabeth and little Jay
Bought two doz. eggs today,
One lb. of cheese,
And nonstick spray
At the Delany St. Café.

Question ? Mark

What is a question mark?

When do you need it?

Where do you put it?

How do you read it?

A question mark is apropos

When there are things you want to know.

You put it after words that ask.

To answer is another's task.

A present for me?
Can I give it a squeeze?
Can I pull off the ribbons?
Can I open it, please?

Exclamation Point

The exclamation point has clout.

HIP! HIP! HOORAY!

STRIKE THREE! YOU'RE OUT!

It fires you up, there is no doubt.

The symbol means you have to SHOUT!

Annie crawled under
When she heard the thunder,
Along with some dust and a spider.
KA-BOOM!
There's nothing more frightening
Than listening to lightning,
Unless it's that spider beside her.
EEEK! EEEK!

Comma

The comma is common
And commonly used
To separate clauses
With essential pauses.

Don't want to confuse you,
But think you should know,
It does not say "Stop."
It simply says "Slow."

Please use it whenever
You're writing the date,
Words in a series,
And cities with states.

Today, March 1,
I boarded a train
In sleet, snow, and rain
For Bar Harbor, Maine.

Apostrophe

Alas, the poor apostrophe
Has two big jobs, it seems to me.
In order to help words possess,
It tags along and adds an "s"
(Like Mickey's mess or Della's dress).

And when one word, not two, is better,
It happily replaces letters.
Whatever's left is not a fraction.
We'll call the new word a contraction
(Like can't or we'll or it's or she'll).

Mickey made a mighty mess,
Spilling paint on Della's dress.
Now it's being washed and pressed.

"Quotation Marks"

Quotation marks come two by two.

Use two before, two when you're through.

Enclosed are words said by another,

Like, *"Clean this messy room!"* yelled Mother.

Or

"Fourscore and seven years ago . . ."

Who said those words?

I'll bet you know!

"Four-score and seven years ago..."
Abraham Lincoln
"You were right!"

Colon

The colon is quite stubborn,
And always will insist
It be the one and only one
To introduce a list.

Another use, when telling time,
No matter how you spin it,
At 6:30 it separates
The hours from the minutes.

6:30

I shook my blue jeans upside down.
Both pockets emptied, these I found:
Some cookie crumbs, a plastic spoon,
A box of raisins from last June,
Two gum balls, and a red balloon.
We'd better wash my blue jeans soon!

Semicolon

The semicolon separates
Two sentences, if they relate.

Tomorrow's my birthday; I'm going to be seven.

I'm having a party at half past eleven.

Ten friends are invited; I am so excited!

Parentheses

Parentheses' two hands are gentle,
Enclosing words that aren't essential.

At lunch, my friends asked me to trade
My chocolate milk for lemonade,
My super sub (from Barney's deli)
For pita bread with gloppy jelly.
My deviled eggs (Mom makes the best)
For sour grapes (that I detest).
Mom always told us we should share.
Tomorrow I'm not sitting there!

Ellipsis points . . . three tiny dots . . .

Are perfect for those silent spots.

Their use, dear reader, is permitted

When certain phrases are omitted.

Well . . . I wonder . . . could it be

That rainbows come out just for me?

Dash

The dash—a punctuation mark—
Is more casual than a comma.
So I prefer to think it is
A comma in pajamas!

Oops! I had better mention this.
Remember when you read it,
A dash is used to emphasize
The words that will precede it.

One thing I must tell you—
Not one, there are two—
I'm glad I am me,
And I'm glad you are you!

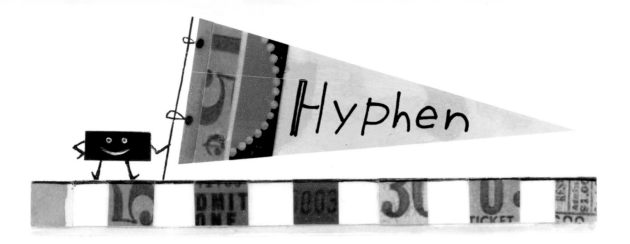

Hyphen

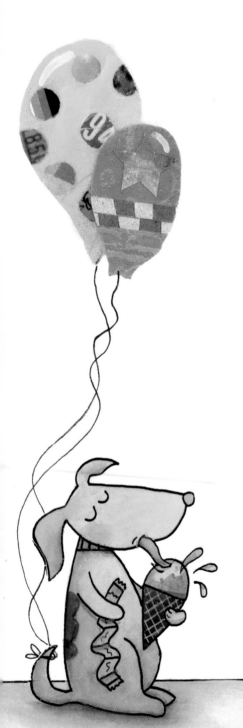

Don't let hyphen fool you.
A dash, it is not.
This poem will remind you,
In case you forgot.

To form compound words
It sometimes is found
Like tom-tom and T-shirt,
And merry-go-round.

Also you should know, some-
times it will appear
And split up a word when
A line end is near.

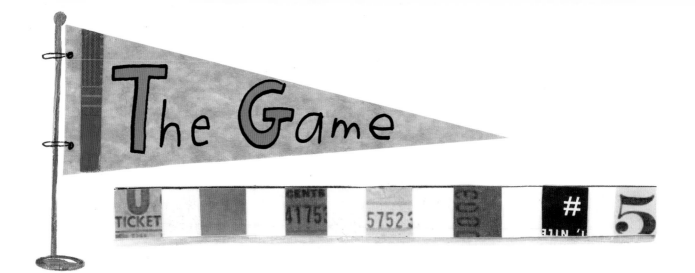

The Game

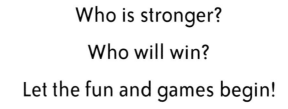

Who is stronger?

Who will win?

Let the fun and games begin!

But period was soon to fall.

It happened when it kicked the ball.

First it tripped and then it plopped

And that is when the playing stopped.

Words took note and congregated.

Soon a sentence was created.

One by one, each punctuation

Ran to its preferred location.

Sentences were dancing, laughing,

Joining hands, and paragraphing.

Words went whirling by, enraptured.
Paragraphs were being chaptered.

And, with not a word to spare,
Stories piled up everywhere!

Happy fans rushed from the stands.
All were cheering, clapping hands.

the game and win together!

When the dust cleared it revealed
Readers on the playing field!

Mixing words and punctuation—
It's a winning combination!

tion Celebration?

To Nicholas, Peter, Alex, Annie, Meg, and Scotty
—E.K.B

To Bailey and Chelsea
—J.W.

Henry Holt and Company, LLC, *Publishers since 1866*
175 Fifth Avenue, New York, New York 10010 [www.HenryHoltKids.com]

Henry Holt ® is a registered trademark of Henry Holt and Company, LLC.
Text copyright © 2009 by Elsa Knight Bruno
Illustrations copyright © 2009 by Jenny Whitehead
All rights reserved.
Distributed in Canada by H. B. Fenn and Company Ltd.

Library of Congress Cataloging-in-Publication Data
Bruno, Elsa Knight.
Punctuation celebration / Elsa Knight Bruno ; illustrated by Jenny Whitehead.—1st ed.
p. cm.
ISBN 978-0-8050-7973-9
1. English language—Punctuation—Juvenile literature. I. Whitehead, Jenny. II. Title.
PE1450.B726 2009   428.2—dc22   2008018337

First Edition—2009
The artist used gouache and cut paper on 90-lb. Arches watercolor
paper to create the illustrations for this book.
Printed in September 2010 in China by South China Printing Company Ltd.,
Dongguan City, Guangdong Province, on acid-free paper. ∞

5 7 9 10 8 6

Concession Stand!